Voices Extended

Neil Paul
Sheldon H. Clark

VOICES EXTENDED

Copyright © 2016, 2021 by Neil Paul and Sheldon H. Clark

First published in 2016. Reissued with minor emendations in 2021.

Distributed to the trade by Rock's Mills Press
www.rocksmillspress.com

Preface

The writers of these poems happened to meet recently and in conversation recognized that their poetic interests and ideals were compatible – and that they were both drawn to themes inspired by Nature and Religion. Moreover, both of them had quite recently published collections of poetry: Neil Paul's A Slim Volume (2009) and Sheldon Clark's Poetry and Prayer Sketches (2013).

They have now collaborated to present this selection of recent poems. Neither has in any way compromised his vision or technique. Both poets express their thoughts and emotions succinctly and memorably. Sheldon Clark's poems are forcefully direct, often focus sharply on religious themes, and frequently use repetition to strengthen emotion. Neil Paul's poems are characteristically quieter and apparently simple, restrained, as they soberly observe and comment on the natural and familial.

Brought together in one volume, these two sets of poems complement each other effectively, deepening meaning and strengthening the pleasure they can give to attentive readers.

Alan Bishop, D. Phil.
Professor Emeritus
McMaster University

Acknowledgements

We gratefully acknowledge the contributions to this volume of poems made by The Reverend Canon Robert Brownlie, Joan A. Clark, Cynthia Croll, Shauna Doracin, The Reverend John Lockyer, Priscilla Reeve, Gail Gauvreau, and Ed VandenDool, whose voices extended our own. Our prayer is that the readers will also share their voices and be part of our mystical choir.

Thank you,
Sheldon & Neil

Poems

by

Neil Paul

Cold Stone and Snow

Cold stone and snow
Seem far away
From summer's warmth
And happy day.

Lord, give us eyes
To see the light
On snow filled days
Or winter night.

The Breeze

The breeze in the leaves
Beckons us,
To see the light within.

Tulips

I heard the tulips sing today
Their mouths
Toward the sun.

Their melody was pure and clean,
For they had just begun
To celebrate
Their journey
From deep within the soil.

I glanced towards them
Evening time,
Their shadows
Stretching long.

Their petals gently closed again
To end
Their daily song.

The echoes lingered
Lovingly.
I felt my heart grow strong.

Family

I hear the furnace
Rattle in the night.
It forms a spiral
Of retreating time.

Back... back... back still
To dark bleak
Sleepless nights.

I am an actor fumbling
On the stage.

Stumbling to leave the script
Whose words no longer give direction.

Arms reach out
I stumble past detection.

The furnace coughs
Returning time affirms
A new, new script
Asserting clear direction.

The stage gives footing
As the words flow free.

The furnace memory fades
And yet —

I hear my sister crying in the wind.
I burn a memory on my father's grave.

Firewood

Gnarled with rough bark
This warms me without burning.

The promise kindles: loud and clear I hear

"You will be warmed by me."

Wood has a language that has weight.

The future tense in words…
Not its first language,

Weight… grain… scent

Speak of substance without speaking.

History is whispered here:
"I leaned into the wind
felt heat, drought, rain
yet never counted pain
worth moving for…"

The warmth…
the promised warmth…
sustaining warmth
against advancing cold.

The wood that burns…
the wood—the Word,
burns without consuming.

Lizard

Sleeping so softly
In the warm noon sun,
The eyelid flits—
Takes in the wharf
For predators or prey.

Within the ribcage
Dwells no fear;
And though rage
Flashes,
Sudden,
From his liquid tongue,
It is contained.

That lizard heart
That lizard brain…
They sleep so softly
Yet
They threaten pain.

Fire

The fire of desire
Glows with elusive flame.

The slice of cheese upon the tongue
anticipates
the slice to come.

The satisfaction of the meal
is yet so fleeting
that we feel… again
the urge to eat.

We greet each day
with new desire.

Hands to the fence's wire
we gaze from our distorted world
and trace a sunbeam
to its golden source.

The Ladies

All the ladies in their eighties
Are delighted when I come;
And I greet them with a curious delight.

In the land of the demented
There are things that are resented;
And not paying strict attention sure is one.

They will whack you with their wheelchair
To determine if you do care;
Then they'll tilt their head and coyly catch your eye.

It's the smile that tugs the heart-strings
And the wonder that the face brings;
For the face reflects the journey that's been long.

So you shake their hands and gather
Even though you think you'd rather,
Be away to do a hundred other things.

Yet that journey—oh that journey
What a wondrous, wondrous journey,
As you catch refracted glimpses of their life.

They're still dealing—they're still feeling
All the joys and all the conflicts,
Of their strife.

And I wonder what they're seeing
As they contemplate their being,
And they navigate the homestretch of their life.

Dinner Time

One table – several faces
The eye remembers
And the heart records.

Bringing the past to present
Voices whisper... faces form again
Odd phrases, once forgotten, return again.

Roast beef... potatoes
Lettuce and tomatoes
Move from hand to hand
Spiraling...
Drawing other hands.

Suddenly
The heart is flooded, luminous, filled.

Multifaceted faces form the One
The One
Who walks beside us in the dark
Absorbs the terror
When the terror comes
And holds the door against the wind.

Ear-eye-the nose and tongue
Have ushered in—from memory's corridors
For heart to see—the One.

Overheard

"When hell freezes over!"

The terse tone of the passing stranger
Flashed the words—
Unmitigated rage…

And though not meant for me
The potion lingered
With its cold resolve.

What brings a person to such resolution?
Anger?
Guilt?
Regret?

When these three meet
Their potency increases.

Memories refuse to focus:
Colours
Shapes
Forms
Come to a stop.

They spin the mind 'til syllables refract.
Blood thickens.
Words decompose.

Dark deeds divulge intentions undefined.

The sullen rage that freezes all perception
Draws a cold curtain
Then withdraws the soul.

So there's the pain
The cooling hell that freezes
The evanescent self
Trapped in its own deceit.

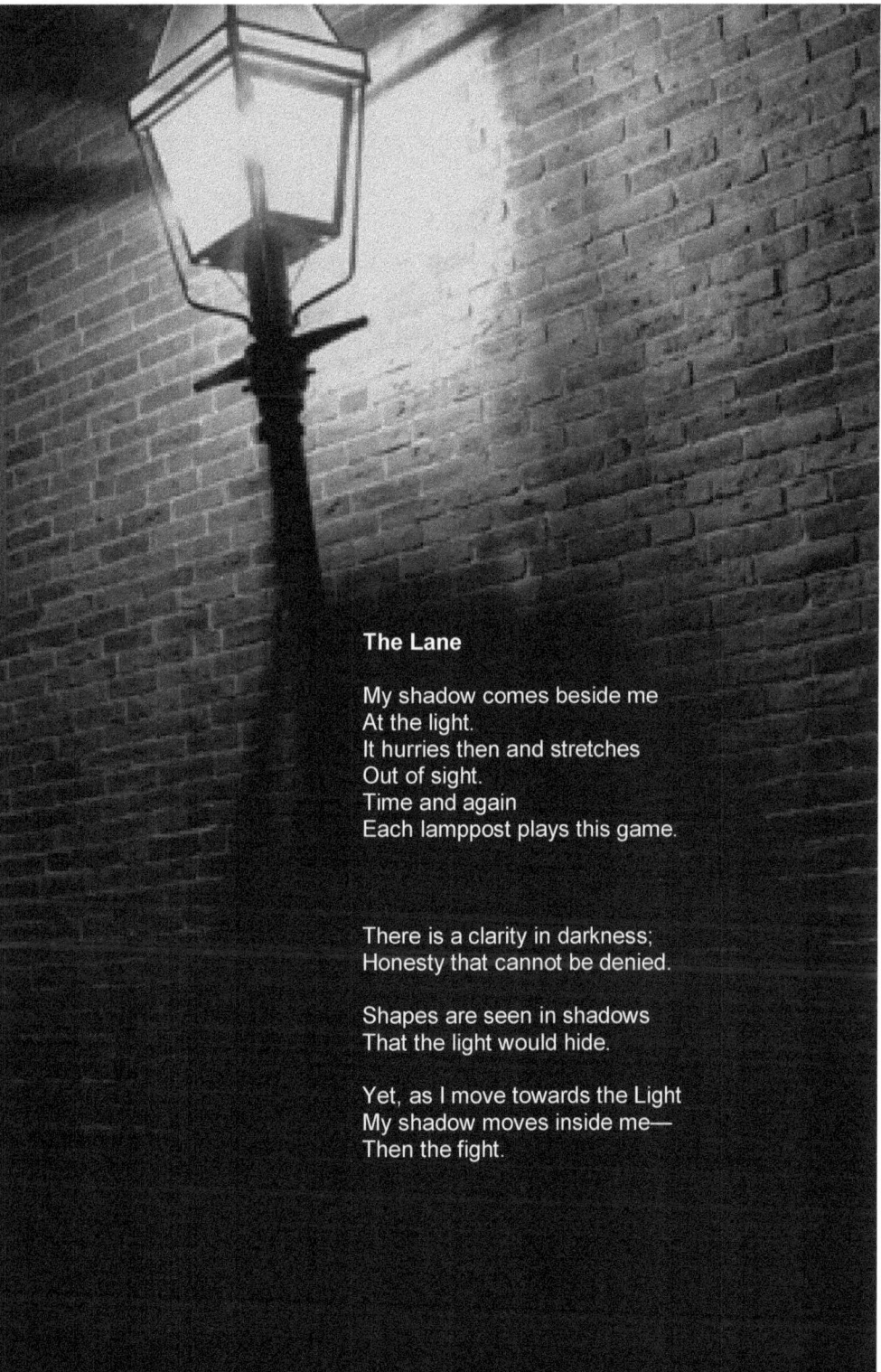

The Lane

My shadow comes beside me
At the light.
It hurries then and stretches
Out of sight.
Time and again
Each lamppost plays this game.

There is a clarity in darkness;
Honesty that cannot be denied.

Shapes are seen in shadows
That the light would hide.

Yet, as I move towards the Light
My shadow moves inside me—
Then the fight.

Heat

The three who walked into the furnace
Knew no fear.

I know no fire,
Yet know the fear
That kindles at resolve
When
Clear conviction beckons,
Plans unfold,
Revelations tumble
From the heart.

The oxygen of that old furnace
Flares coals to flame.

Let resolutions burn.
Let all convictions
Plans
And revelations
Take the heat…

Blackbird

The blackbird shows red colour
When he flies.

Perched on the bending reed
His black coat gleams.

Fretting with others in the rush-filled swamp
He blends—shows just a hint of flame.

"Again… Again… I whisper…
….   Fly again."

Ode to Manfred

He paws the ground.
He snorts the air.
He surveys his domain.
He licks his flank.
He snorts again
And shrugs
His coal black mane.

There had been bulls
Before he came
And other bulls did follow.
Yet Manfred's praise
Through all his days
Makes other praise
Sound hollow.

His black was midnight black
And blacker.
And though he never rushed his cows
He never was a slacker.

He seemed to know his owner's step
Regardless of direction.
And could it be that those dark eyes
Gave back a clear reflection?

Now Manfred's gone,
But the owner stayed.
He loved the land you see.
And instead of grooming Manfred's hide
It's greens and fairways
For you and me.

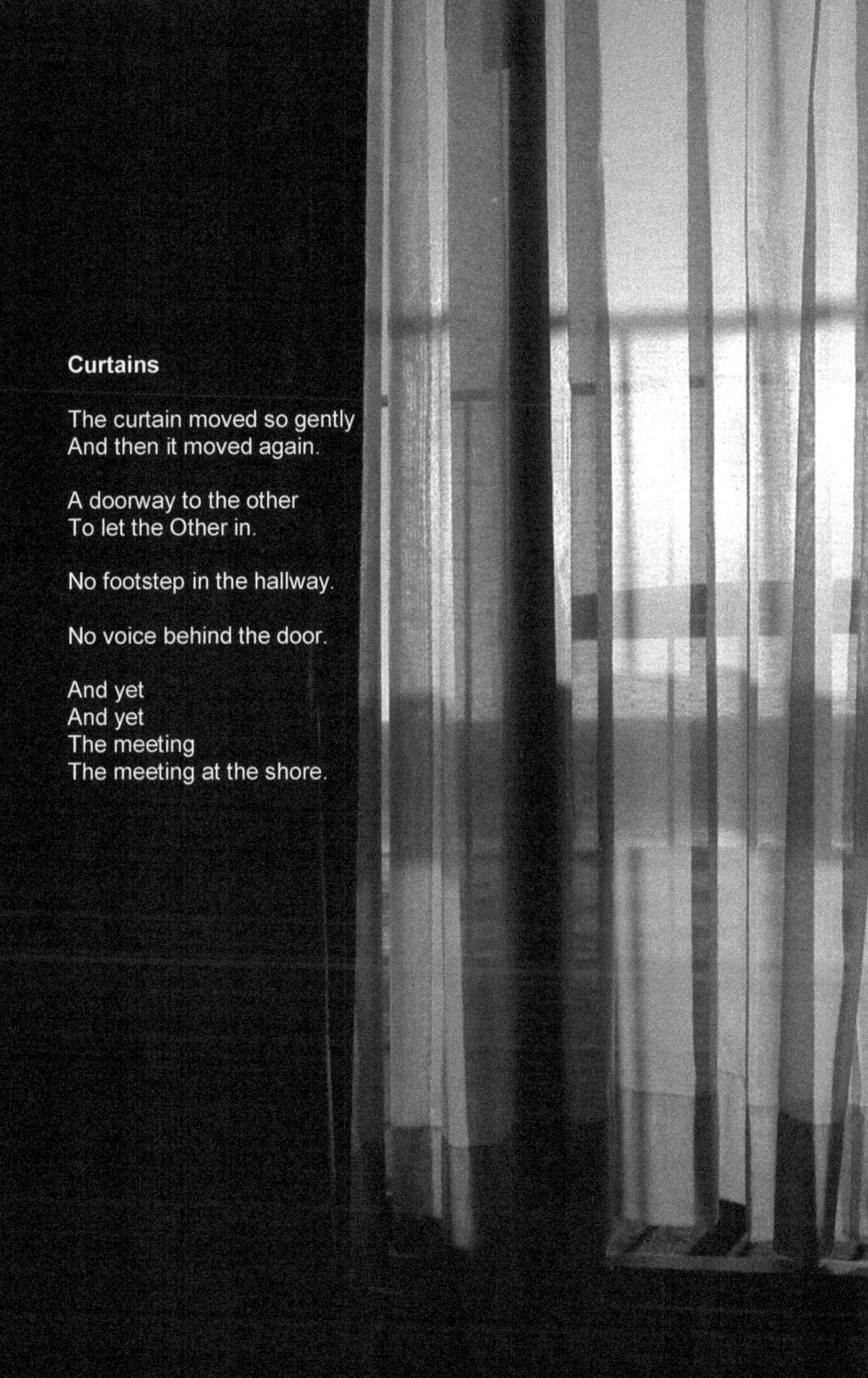

Curtains

The curtain moved so gently
And then it moved again.

A doorway to the other
To let the Other in.

No footstep in the hallway.

No voice behind the door.

And yet
And yet
The meeting
The meeting at the shore.

Leaves

A leaf retains its structure when it falls.

One last impression
On the sidewalk damp.

The oak leaf lifts its points in glad farewell.

Serrated edges of the beech
Retain their crisp design.

The maple shows its pointed mountain range.

Now is the time
To savour every line.

Poems

by

Sheldon H. Clark

Hawk Gone in Snow Fog

Hawk gone in snow fog
Crystal bulrushes and grass
Spring almost winked

Accept Me

Accept me.
Love me.
Forgive me.

Accept me as I am.
Love me, as I am, toes to head and down again.
Forgive my trespasses.
Show justice, mercy, humility.

Accept me.
Love me.
Forgive me.

Accept my race, creed, colour,
Caucasian, Mongolian, Negroid, outer space,
White, brown, yellow, aqua marine,
This ism, that ism, and other isms that isms make.

Accept me.
Love me.
Forgive me.

Love me simply for the fact, I am.
Love me for the truth, you are.
Love me, as I am alone, and we are together.
Love without tenses.

Accept me.
Love me.
Forgive me.

Forgive me. Justice is peace.
Forgive me. Mercy is everlasting.
Forgive me. Truth endures.

Accept me.
Love me.
Forgive me.

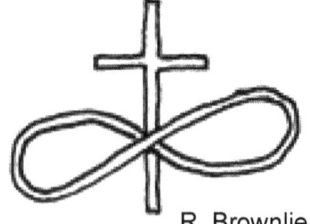

R. Brownlie

R. Brownlie

The Moon Leans Like This

And the moon leans like this off to one side
Not perfectly positioned
But present pronounced secure.

And the moon leans like this to one side,
Elliptical oval light shadow,
Beaming a muted ray.

The moon leans like this, reclining
To share the bed time story, the pillow,
Comfortable and loving.

The moon leans like this
Arching, stretching, yawning, sighing
To the bye-baby-bunting who takes
But a single breath, and then
Sleeps behind a cloud.

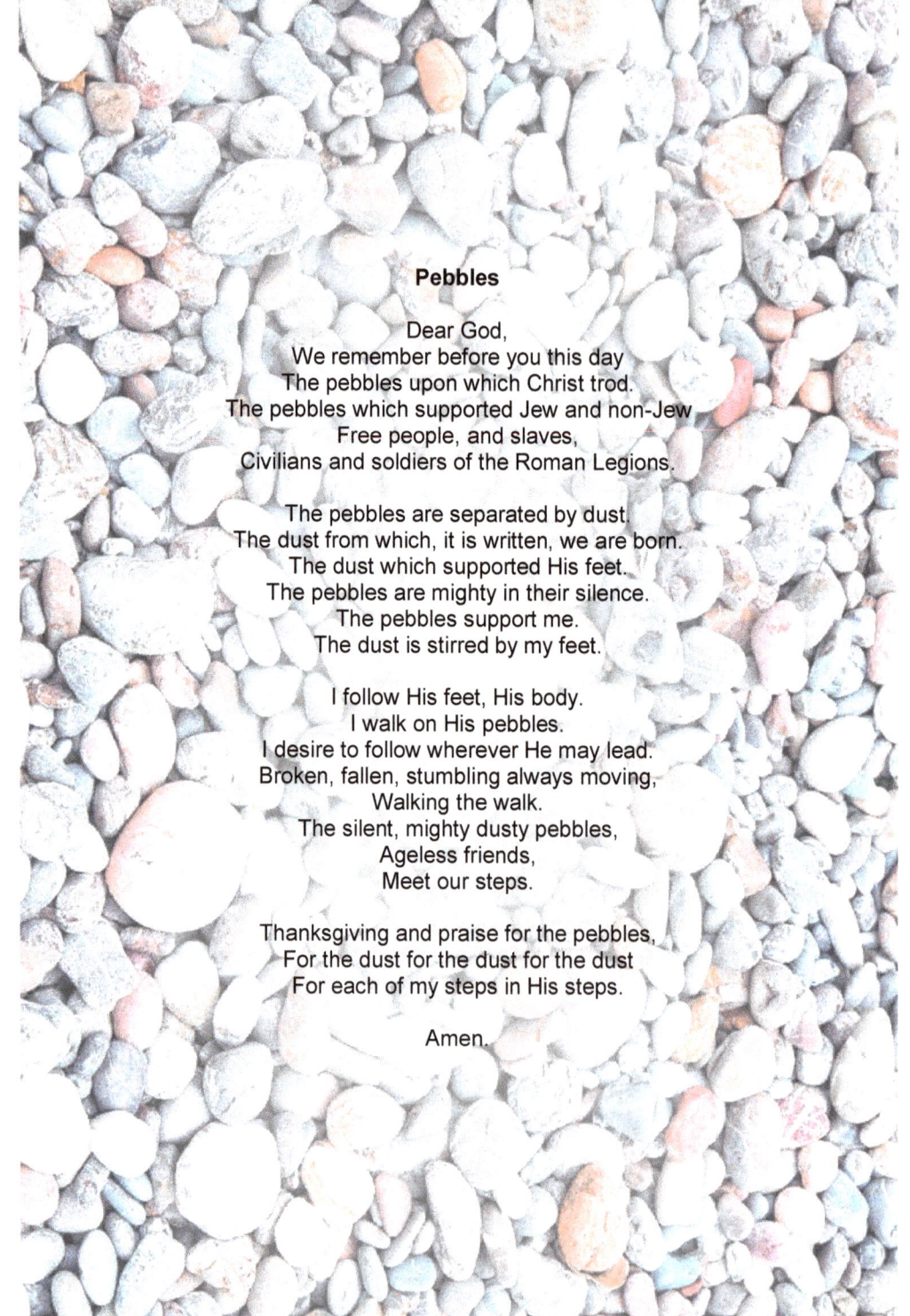

Pebbles

Dear God,
We remember before you this day
The pebbles upon which Christ trod.
The pebbles which supported Jew and non-Jew
Free people, and slaves,
Civilians and soldiers of the Roman Legions.

The pebbles are separated by dust.
The dust from which, it is written, we are born.
The dust which supported His feet.
The pebbles are mighty in their silence.
The pebbles support me.
The dust is stirred by my feet.

I follow His feet, His body.
I walk on His pebbles.
I desire to follow wherever He may lead.
Broken, fallen, stumbling always moving,
Walking the walk.
The silent, mighty dusty pebbles,
Ageless friends,
Meet our steps.

Thanksgiving and praise for the pebbles,
For the dust for the dust for the dust
For each of my steps in His steps.

Amen.

Mary Simply Smiled

Mary Simply smiled.
No Mona Lisa enigmatic questing, here.
Just a lovely smile.

I gazed at her sunshine and was temporarily blind-sided,
And saw in my Damascus' eye, her black eyes, a lash winking,
And the rounded cheeks speaking eloquently.

Mary simply smiled,
Innocently, as Eve might smile a caress to a sunbeam.
Really, a lovely smile.

The shadow from the sun evoked love, peace, life, tranquility.
Mary's smile was the seductive product of spiritual wholeness.
A lovely smile.

I gazed at the beauty in the manger,
Almost hidden in the bedded straw,
And, perceived a stillness of wonderment at
Mary's child-to-Child gaze.
That lovely smile.

Mary simply smiled.
No intelligible speech required or necessary.
Just a lovely smile.

Mary simply smiled.
My new eyes followed Mary's gaze to her Child
And back to mine again.
Just a lovely smile.

June 6, 1944 ~ June 6, 2014, 70th Anniversary, D-Day

The Convicted

The Convicted
   soldiers died by the hundreds of thousands
   In "Dress Rehearsals" and on "Normandy's Beaches."
   Across six continents, 'round the Pacific, just <u>not</u> Antarctica.
   Real people died. Everywhere children died
   On Land, Sea, and in the Sky.

The Convicted
   conscientious objectors survived penitentiaries,
   hospitals, civilian public service camps.
   Those COs were ostracized by the majority as cowards, subversives, traitors,
   but they, too, were loved by family, friends, fellow prisoners of conscience,
   patients, and buddies.
   They were 'safe', hidden away
   As poisonous insinuations the system denied.
   COs were dead for all intents and purposes - a matter of expediency.

The Convicted
   soldiers sometimes survived to pay homage to the dead.
   they became comrades in arms, friends, and wartime lovers, even married.
   Their latter day every day abundances speak eloquently about ideals,
   Will Power, Daring do, "The Ultimate Sacrifice."

The Convicted
   released, cared for the incarcerated,
   physical, emotional and mental casualties;
   Disfigured reconstructions, collateral damage
   Weakened by brave wounds time does not heal.
   Soldier and CO both became heroic witnesses
   To loyalties ideals, values, Truth, and unconditional love.

The Convicted
  Once were distinct voices, poles apart,
  Remembered their time, overcame their fears,
  And found personal salvation as a single voice.
  They went beyond patriotic rhetoric
  Into the common life song of Being and Becoming,
  Once separately, then, together.

And they shall beat their swords into ploughshares.
                                              Isaiah 4:2

Angelo/Angela

Angelo, oblivious to being an instrument of God's will,
Nonchalantly, and in need of relief
Unwittingly trespassed
Into space belonging to others and produced anger.

Angela, aware of being an instrument of God's will,
Knowingly expanded her personal space
To discover she included
Room enough for strangers and produced love.

Their trespasses somersaulted into,
Do unto others, as you would have others do unto you.
Blessed are the peacemakers:
for they shall be called the children of God.

Once upon a time
Lions and mice kept apart,
Until a snared Leo needed some small sharp teeth
To gnaw apart his hempen trap and become free.

Once free the lion understood another Truth.
The original mouse trespass of lion space,
Was but obedient witness to a higher Law:
"Little friends may prove to be great friends."

Faith is a state of being.
It is garnered by mercy; not force and violence.
Faith is the providence of great strength found
In letting go and being surprised by
The sublime power of weakness and vulnerability.

Now faith is the substance of things hoped for,
the evidence of things not seen.

Hebrews 11:1

Her Smile

Her smile causes others to respond in kind.
She smiles in response to another's greeting.

She sleeps a great deal.

"Silence is golden,"
yet her facial expressions and body language communicate,
"Hello." "No." "Yes!" "Okay." "I don't want to."
"Let's go."

Graciousness is not forgotten.

"I love you,"
will illuminate a turn of her head
and the focus of her eyes.
Silently, it is as though she queries:
"Do you really mean what you say?"

"I want to go now."

Her secret word/world is safe, locked up, mixed with the Eternal.

The Parable of the Mustard Seed

The Second Adam sowed mustard seed in a field.
The seeds' husks held the power of potential extravagance
Potent grains to dispel death, decay, darkness,
enmity, evil, fear, limitation.
Potent grains to dispense love, joy, peace,
goodness, faith, meekness, temperance.

The mustard seed emerged from darkness to Light.
Rooted firmly, it sprouted to magnificent stature.
The seeds endings marked the openings for abundance.
Joyful songsters miraculously alighted, rested, built nests
and raised their young.

Then, they flitted away, and away, and ever back again.
They announced the Good News: "God is good."
We, the living seeds, flourish
To disperse the fruit of the Spirit.

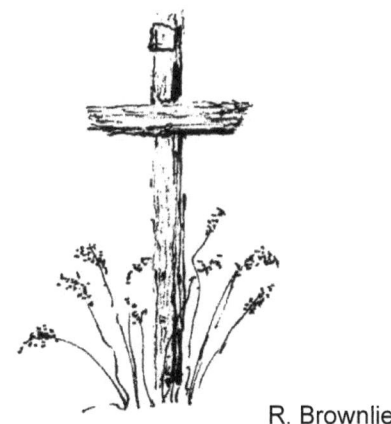

R. Brownlie

On Prayer and the Cross

Let us pray,
Dear God, we come before Thee today, as though for the first time.
We are Newborn this day, this Good Friday, this day of prayer.

In our prayer
We remember before Thee, Thy Son.
We remember Thy love for us through Him.

In our prayer
We cry out for Forgiveness and Grace.
We are all One in Christ.

In our prayer
We remember His Agony on the Cross.
It is there we encounter His forgiveness for us.

In our prayer
Dear God, we Crucify with Him old thoughts and behaviours,
The very attitudes and actions that keep us apart from Thee.

In our prayer
We anticipate the Resurrection, New Birth, Eternal Life,
Through Thy unconditional love for us.

In our prayer we need Thy Light,
Thy Strength and Thy companionship to express Thy Love,
The Love Christ taught to each of us to give to one another.

Amen.

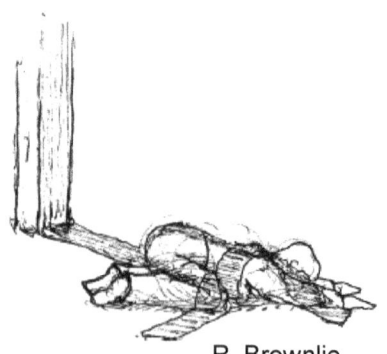

R. Brownlie

Demons

Subcutaneous welts lift surface skin uncomfortably
Scratching, pin-pointing, crablike movements,
Traumatizing, tantalizing, torturing, tormenting.

Mental welts produce nerve and spider webbing
Altering, shifting, visionary thought processes
Causing depressions, dejections, despondencies, desolation.

Demon tumors of pain attack body and spirit,
Seek, demand, cry out for
Relief, release, removal, redress.

Demons external and internal
Insidious parasites feeding fueling agony,
Relentless scourges devouring comfort, even existence itself.

I am a Christian

I am a Christian

This is a provocative statement in today's world.
Maybe, it has always been provocative
To claim to live a certain way of life.
I exist.
I am the sum of my limitations.

The Christ I know is present in life and in death.
Christ is Divine Love.
Images push onion layers of human and natural happenings;
Not all pleasant /unpleasant.
I exist to love.
I learn to love unconditionally, even so-called enemies,
As Christ did.

No minimalism, itemization, definition.
The miniscule produces frustration.
Give water. Clothe, feed someone something.
No excuses. Go make the visit.
Turn to Eternal Silence.
God/Christ/Spirit is found not wanting.

No. "There Am I."
Earth, Sea, Sky, Light, Night.
Yes, the Eternal.
I exist.
I AM is beyond limitation.

I am a Christian in spite of evidence to the contrary.
Even as He sees that I am held captive by skin and bones.
Even as he liberates me through His Grace.

Pat's Case

Pat's case isn't complicated: Alzheimer's / Dementia
Pat says: "*I don't know,*" a lot.
"Had any lately?"
Honest fragile handsome blue-eyed answer:
                                                                 "*I don't know*".

Pat's case isn't complicated.
When asked, "Hey, Patrick. How ya doin'?"
Eyes piercing a forlorn horizon, He replies:
                                                                 "*I don't know*".

Pat's case isn't complicated.
Beautiful day? Blue skies? Green grass? What's in a day?
Yesterday's detritus gone.
The faded white-haired six foot Leprechaun whispers:
                                                                 "*I don't know*".

Pat's case isn't complicated.
Hear that robin's song wafting on the breeze?
Head to one side listening. Hands busy. Feet shuffling.
Then, the soft:
                                                                 "*I don't know*".

Pat's case isn't complicated.
The feel of your horse's muzzle is wonderful?
Apologetically, even secretly:
                                                                 "*I don't know*".

Pat's case isn't complicated.
Coffee? Tea? Guinness? Quite refreshing.
Lips slightly parted:
                                                                 "*I don't know*".

Pat's case isn't complicated.
Pardon? What did you say? Times passages?
Shyly:
                                    "*I love Molly, for sure This I do know*".

Pat's case isn't complicated.
Two children: Charles and Colleen.
Ireland. Canada. Bally D. Farm. Horses. Fun. Hard work.
All in a day?
                                                                 "*I don't know*".

Pat's Case isn't complicated: Alzheimer's / Dementia.
Pat says: "I don't know," a lot.
Had any lately?
                                                                 "*I don't know*".

R. Brownlie

Someone Opens an Orange in Silence

Someone opens an orange in silence at a sidewalk café.

She cradles the globed fruit with loving hands,
Folded umbilical looking out expectantly, and
Cointreau induced saliva
Moistened lips
Prepare.

Human apertures
Gently separate the engorged skin,
Reveal the hidden core,
The emerging freshness
Nature does the rest.

Juice squirts its tenderness without
Within a tissue tears to release
The half, the quarter, the crescent moons.

This *ménage a deux,*
Is as slow steady silent
As the birthing of a foal at midnight.

Wet hands lift newborn fruit to tongue
To taste to emulsify to ingest in God's sweet order.

Politely, passersby avert their eyes,
Curious
To smell to touch to taste
To hear to see
Someone who opens an orange in silence.

R. Brownlie

The Want I Want

The want I want is want is from what want demands.
The want I want is want
From poverty, hunger, injustice, and basic needs.
The want I want is want from physical sickness,
mental sickness, and Spiritual disease.
The want I want is want from lies, innuendo, falsehoods, half-truths.

Wealth and poverty, nothing and plenty, excess and deprivation,
Even-Stephen unfairness, infinite much and finite little, all want.
Bodies, minds, souls, want.
Food, clothing, shelter wants fill nomadic meanderings
Across deserts to mountaintops,
Down into the shadows of evil.

Search wants John and Jane Doe's wherever, whenever, forever.

Loss wants to be found.
Grief wants to end.
Death itself, is transfigured by want.
God and the Devil want.

The want-lists want obedience, innocence, loyalty, dedication, creation,
Atmospheres, black holes, quantitative analysis, dimensions, erasures,
Opportunities, hopefulness, kindness, friendship,
Instinct, order, randomness,
And especially faith, hope, and love.

The want-lists are not wanting for want.

They are the endless identifications of what could be.
If only the insatiable could become sated
And put an end
To want.

It Was By Happenstance I Caught A Glimpse In The Mirror

It was by happenstance I caught a glimpse in the mirror.
Just walking past and there was this figure,
Not frightening, but casually night-light enshrouded.
It was right to left, top to bottom, myself.
Suspended there, caught sightless,
Conjured ragged space flotsam.
Silence uttered not a word.
No escape from naked reality.
Sagged, wrinkled, not a patch of mental hero.
Experience beckoned.

Congenial arms welcomed.
Darkness prevailed.
Befriended, renewed, and made whole.
Transitory illusion disappeared;
Was replaced by a momentary inescapable ecstasy of sheer joy, wonder, and awe.

CJ's Fox Hunt

"Fox Hunting is a misnomer." Charles James leads the Chase.
"Frivolity 'cross country, more likely the case."

Twilight time, Charles James woke to a brave dawn,
Dew crested fields, cool breeze, and whispering spirits
Among the forest folk.

Bird song called. Deer lifted chiseled heads, and then grazed again.
A lone skunk stopped to sniff, listen, and then shuffle away.

CJ stretched, yawned, and padded black paws derived from russet legs,
broke slowly his covert.
"Plenty of time for horses, hounds, and people to drink spirits."

CJ padded to the edge of the easterly Dufferin fence line, watched,
Satisfied in the misty turn out.
Ever–patient horses, soft voices,
and occasional hounds gave faint impressions of the Chase to be.

"Mixed pack," CJ ruminized. "Bitches, dog hounds, geldings, mares,
And scarlet, black, rat-catcher."
"Mixed pack. No bitches in heat. Pity."

"Master, please." MFH doffed cap. Artillery voice resonated:
"When Hunting, pay heed to horn, tongue, shaky bushes, and the View."

CJ ready steadied for the Chase.
He pledged himself to evaporate into thin air.
Assembled.
Off they moved at a fast trot across the stone road to the woods.

Toot. Toot. "They're off." Harness jangled. Hooves beat. Thuds. Grunts.
Silence echoed from birch and maple against opposing Bathurst Hill.

The Field strung out, ranked by happenstance,
Subscription distinction of no concern.
CJ jumped on the top split rail, paused, saw them focus attention, and leapt.

"There he goes." Horn doubled.
Huntsman, MFH, and Field galloped forward, ever forward.
Cross Mar-vel Creek.
Found along the opposing split rail.
Scent filled field, air and wood.

"I know of ground bees," CJ calculated. "It'll be wonderful."
Three beat canter. Up and Over. "Heels down. Heads up. Knees in."
Riding school tight.

Cross Mar-vel Creek. Up Bathurst Hill. Along Sugar Bush Trail.
"Whack." Winter's deadfall surprised first followers. "'Ware branch!"
Ah. Too late.

Second flight heard, sensed the stir, then out of nowhere, a string of stings.
Well-bred horses felt loose reins, and high jinxed into the surrounding bush.

"'Ware bees!" Too late! "Damn the consequences. CJ again!"
CJ doubled back, enjoying the pandemonious undulating dislocations of a spontaneous St Vitus' Dance.

"Wonderful. Wonderful. Wonderful.
That'll teach 'em to try to out fox the fox,"
CJ chortled with unmitigated joy.

"There he goes." Undulations ceased.
Control authoritatively exercised its right.
CJ waited for the multitudes to be in view.

"There he goes."
CJ trotted, strolled, tantalized, and teased from Bathurst Hill.
Fancy, lead bitch, nosed the scent. Gave tongue.
"They're off," CJ smiled in satisfaction.

"To the knoll. To the knoll. To the knoll.
"Westward the way," CJ loved to lead the Chase.
Along Sugar Bush Trail, jump coops, mud slide,
swamp path, road stones. Live for Livery Hill.

Away. Away. Away. Over logs, staggered jumps,
surprising trail twists. Up West Dufferin slope.
"To the knoll. To the knoll.
Plenty of holes. Disappear."
CJ fox-laughed out loud.

Horn doubled. Hounds cried. "All on." Huntsman, "Hello-ed."
Determination everywhere.
Sun rays filtered through mature trees.
Pines wavered. Astonished.

CJ flashed. Disappeared. Simply wasn't anymore.
On west Dufferin Knoll , beyond Livery Hill, fading maples
and dark pine, hounds milled, mystified.
Huntsman called, "Gone to ground." Master halted
Field assembled. "We'll give 'im best, today."

CJ exhilarated, circled, enjoyed the march past from
his lofty protected vantage.
He stretched, yawned, and padded black paws
derived from russet legs, viewed 'em from his covert.

Plenty of time for horses, hounds, and people to drink in the spirits.

"Gone away."
CJ stretched, yawned, and padded black paws out of russet legs,
"Mice are also nice and will suffice."

Grief Hurts

Grief hurts.
Pure and simple, grief hurts

Strong and weak, faint-hearted and courageous
Succumb cry and fight for emotional control.

Time, place, condition, circumstance are of no matter
Grief hurts in the here and now, right now. *Jesus wept.*

Grief is not an identity.
It is the emotive questing to live through the pain of absence.

Yet, like Lazarus being called forth from the tomb
The grave clothes of grief can be unbound.

Faith and time work their healing powers
Plumbing another dimension to love.

Grief hurts.

www.ingramcontent.com/pod-product-compliance
Lightning Source LLC
Chambersburg PA
CBHW051120110526
44589CB00026B/2989